YOU
WOULDN'T
TELL YOUR MOTHER

MIKE ROSS

Strathearn Publishing
TRADE DISTRIBUTION
foulsham
The Publishing House, Bennetts Close,
Cippenham, Berks. SL1 5AP

strathearn publishing ltd.
PO Box 44, Slough, Berkshire, SL1 4YN

ISBN 0-572-01897-5

Copyright © 1993 M. F. Ross

Phototypeset in Great Britain by Typesetting Solutions, Slough.
Printed in Great Britain by Cox & Wyman Ltd., Reading.

Free copy!

We're not getting enough!

And we're certainly not getting it regularly! C'mon guys we need more jokes and one liners. If you don't perform, there won't be a new collection for Christmas '94 — cause I've run out of good ones!

If you hear a funny story and think that it would be good for our next collection, then just send it in.

If we publish *your* joke in the next book, we will acknowledge you as its author and send you a free copy containing your name in print.

You can then flash the book 'round the pub to show how famous you have become. And insist that those who wish to remain in your company buy you drinks in recognition of your achievement!

Yours for a laugh.

ED.
Strathearn Publishing

P.S. You'll find our address on the back of the title page. Where we have more than one submission of the same joke, then it will be the first received which will be given the credit.

5

Q. What do you call a female clown?

A. Clunt!

A white man, stood in a gents toilet wanted to glance down at the cock of the black guy who was standing next to him.

"My God," he exclaimed and looked down blacks . . .

"Yes," said the black man. "When we are young our mothers tie a piece of string to our tool, and then they attach a heavy stone to the string. Eventually that stretches our cocks."

CENSORED

Q. How do you brainwash an Irishman?

6

A. Pee in his wellies.

My Daddy's got two willies!
A small one to do a wee-wee
and a much bigger one
to clean the au pair's teeth!

R. P. — Putney

This guy walks into a Chinese Restaurant.

He's greeted by a very bolshy waiter.

"Sit down — what you want?", says he.

"I'll have chicken and sweet corn soup please."

"And what else?" he says aggressively.

"Uh — chicken chop suey and mixed vegetables."

"What AFTERWARDS?"
says the bloody Chink.

"Apple pie," says our brow-beaten friend.

The food begins to arrive.

The soup is delivered with the waiter's thumb in it.

7

The chicken, too, is deliverd and his thumb is deep into that as well.

Our man keeps his cool and says nothing. Finally the apple pie arrives.

With its arrival, he explodes. "Look here you little bastard, you've had your thumb in every bloody course and now it's covered in custard!"

"Well — I have bad arthritis and my doctor says that I must keep it warm," spat the Chink.

"Yeah — Well why don't you shove it up your arse where it can do something useful."

"In the kitchen when nothing to carry — I do."

John Dodds — Whetstone

I **HATE** THIS KIND OF LANGUAGE —YOU KNOW THAT!

8

Wife The doctor told me that for a forty-year-old I had a fabulous face and body.

Husband And what did he say about your forty-year-old cunt?

Wife Oh. He didn't mention you at all!

A sign in the village store:

CONDOMS FITTED FREE

A customer walked in
and behind the counter saw a
beautiful blonde.

"Are you the girl who fits the
condoms free?

"I certainly am", she said with a
knowing smile.

"Well, you can wash your hands then, I
only want a pound of tomatoes!"

In the vet's waiting room, the Great Dane meets the Terrier.

"What are you in for?"

"The bitch next door was on heat, so I popped over the fence and gave her one! Now I'm here for a castration. What about you?"

10 ▶

"I was passing the bathroom door and saw my mistress bending over the bath. She was stark naked and it was too inviting. I crept up behind her and slipped her a length."

"They're having you put down then are they?" said the Terrier.

"No, no not at all! She brought me in to have my claws trimmed!"

Life's a Bitch
And if you're not very careful
you can marry another!

11

Brian Richards — Mansfield

Q.
How many screws
in a lesbian's coffin?

A.
None!
It's all tongue and
groove.

A blind man waits to cross the road.

His guide dog becomes impatient and pees on his leg.

The man responds by offering food from his pocket.

"That was very understanding," said a fellow pedestrian.

13

"Not a bit," said the blind man.

"When I know where to find his mouth, I can kick him in the balls."

AN AUSTRALIAN CAMEO

"You're a nice looking Sheila!"

"Do ya fuck?"

"I do for smooth talking bastards like you!"

14

Q. What's better than
Roses on your piano?

A. Two lips on your organ!

"Zoo-Keeper, Zoo-Keeper
Your Elephant has fucked my dog."

"That's quite impossible,
show me the dog."

"I can't, I can't
The elephant still has his foot on it."

15

Q. Why did the Arabs
get the oil,
while the Irish got
all the potatoes?

A. The Irish were given
first choice!

The young barmaid was ▓▓▓▓▓▓▓▓ street
when she ▓▓▓▓▓▓▓▓▓▓▓▓▓ small boys
▓▓▓▓▓▓▓▓▓▓ the ▓▓▓▓▓▓
  "What's this ▓▓▓▓▓▓▓ ?" she asked ▓▓▓
▓▓▓▓▓
  " It's a ▓▓▓▓▓▓▓ " replied the boy.
  "Oh, said the barmaid, ▓▓▓▓▓▓▓▓▓ ?"
  "▓▓▓▓▓▓ 'said the boy, ▓▓▓▓▓▓▓ "

16 ▶ *On his first official engagement,
President Clinton rides with the
Queen in a Carriage of State.*

*All of a sudden, the rearmost horse
breaks wind.
Long and wet was the fart by all
accounts.*

*"I do apologise Mr President,"
said the Queen.*

*"That' all right Ma'am," said the
President. "I thought it was the horse!"*

Q. What's the difference
between a goldfish and
a mountain goat?

A. One mucks about in a
fountain, the other ...

17

Then there was the Jewish kamikaze pilot

Crashed his plane into his brother's scrapyard

18

Q. How do you know
who gives good blowjobs?

A. Word of Mouth!

WHADDYA CALL:

Catholics who use the
rhythm method of
birth control?

Mum and Dad!

Two ▮▮▮ were ▮▮▮ their ▮▮▮ when a
naked woman ▮▮▮ and into the woods.
A couple of minutes later she ▮▮▮ two▮▮▮
▮▮▮ and then ▮▮▮ bloke ▮▮▮ two
▮▮▮s of ▮▮▮
Finally followed a little ▮▮▮ up the rear.
The two ▮▮▮ him and ▮▮▮ what
▮▮▮ on.

WHADDYA CALL:

A black necktie salesman?

A tie-coon!

Did you hear about
the Irishman who bought
a toilet brush?

*Two weeks later he was back
to using toilet paper!*

There's a guy stuck in an overseas airport. Trudging round it for the umpteenth time he notices a machine — well tucked away.

On it was an illuminated sign.
 YOUR-WIFE-AWAY-FROM-HOME 25¢
In it was a well positioned hole.

Checking that nobody was looking, he fed in his chopper and inserted 25¢. With great expectations he waited.

20

The machine whirred, it trembled and seem to warm itself.

Then he passed out
in excruciating pain.

When he woke, he was surrounded by a large crowd of giggling people, looking and pointing at his chopper.

The pain returned to confirm his problem and he raised his head to look at his chopper.

There it was, hanging out as he had left it.

With a shirt button sewn on the end!

Q. What's the difference between an oral and a rectal thermomenter?

A. The taste!

22

Q.

Why does Prince Charles have a blue dick?

A.

He stuck it in Di!

Q. Do you believe
in premarital sex?

A. Only if it doesn't
hold up the ceremony!

Q. What's the difference
between ooooh and aaaah?

A. About two inches!

23

A white man stood in a gents toilet ~~chanced~~ to
glance down at the ~~~~ who
was standing ~~~~

"M~~~~ he exclaimed in admiration. "How
do you blokes manage to get such ~~big ones~~?"

"~~Well~~," said the black man. "When w~~~~
our mothers t~~~~ string to ~~~~ tool, and
the~~~~ atta~~~~ heavy stone to the string.
Eventually that stretches our cocks."

"~~Do you know~~, I think I'll try that!" announced
the white man~~~~

A couple of month~~~~
ag~~~~ toilet.

Q. What's hard and dry
on the way in.
Soft and sticky
when it comes out?

A. Chewing gum!

24

DEFINITION:
Piece de resistance:
A French virgin!

The young barmaid was ▓▓▓▓▓▓▓▓ street
when she ▓▓▓▓▓▓▓▓▓▓▓▓▓ small boys
▓▓▓▓▓▓▓▓▓ the ▓▓▓▓▓
"What's this ▓▓▓▓▓?" she asked ▓▓
▓▓▓▓▓▓▓
"It's a ▓▓▓▓▓" replied the boy.
"Oh, said the barmaid, ▓▓▓▓▓▓▓▓"
"▓▓▓▓▓▓▓ 'said the boy, ▓▓▓▓▓▓"

A lady walks into a
hardware store to buy a hinge.
The guy behind the counter says:
"Do you wanna screw for that hinge?"
"No, but I'll blow ya for a toaster!"

So, you want a penis transplant?

25

A black twelve incher costs £2,500!

How much would it cost in white?
That size doesn't come in white!

AND THIS
SHOULD HAVE
BEEN CENSORED
TOO!

A man walks into a doctor's office.

"I'm having a lot of trouble with my penis."

The receptionist becomes flushed and runs out of the room.

The doctor pulls the man aside and says,

"What's the matter with you?

"You don't say things like that!

"First you tell her you have some other problem, then when you come in to see me, you tell *me* about the real problem!"

About a week later, the same man walks in.

This time he announces,

"I'm having trouble with my finger."

The receptionists asks,

"What seems to be the problem?"

"I can't pee through it!"

26

Did you hear the one about the farmer's daughter who couldn't keep her calves together?

27

A woman calls her chauffeur
into her bedroom,

"Now, James, I want you to take off
my blouse!"

Good!

"Now I want you to take off my bra!"

Good!

"Now I want you to take off my panties!"

Very good!

"Now James . . . If I ever catch you
wearing them again, you're fired!"

28

A white man, stood in a gents toilet, chanced to
glance down at the cock of the black guy who
was standing next to him.

"My God," he exclaimed. "Why is your cock
so big?" he asked as he glanced at it's
"Well," said the black man. "When we are young
our mothers tie a piece of string to our tool, and
then they attach a heavy stone to the string.
Eventually that stretches our cocks."

A husband comes out of the bathroom.

He is surprised to see his new wife standing on her head.

"What the hell are you doing?" he says.

"I figured, if you couldn't get it up, you could drop it in!"

How can you tell a second wife?

She's the one with the fake jewellery and real orgasms!

MAN:

Your box is too tight
and your tits are too small.

WOMAN:

Well get off my back!

30

Two Italian homosexuals were
passed by a very handsome
young Sailor.

"Oh what a sweet boy ...
He's good enough to eat!"

"Well you can't Gianni
It's Lent and we've given
up meat."

"Meat yes," said Gianni
"But seafood is OK!"

Little Johnny was caught by his mother having a wank in the bath.

"You mustn't do that to your willy," said she.

"Why not, it's mine and I'll wash it as fast as I like!"

31

What's the difference between a fat girl and a virgin?

One is trying to diet; the other's dying to try it!

Q. Why did God invent alcohol?

A. So fat girls could get laid too!

Did you hear about the guy who was half-Italian and half-Irish?

He'd make you offer you couldn't understand!

32

Q. What's the difference between a hormone and a vitamin?

A. You can't make a vitamin!

Maggie put 'Rest in Peace

But when she

he had

produce

clothin

he had le

told me st

'Till I come

much use

's tombstone.

boasting about

went down.

can see that

tricked by

please stop

rds that

amed nothing

cap.

This one is just too tasteless.

Ed.

On a train journey with his Curate the Bishop struggles with a crossword.

"Three across," says he.

"Exclusively female ...
Four letters ...
Ends in UNT?"

33

"That would be AUNT" said the curate.

"Well yes, that would fit too!" said the Bishop.

"Have you got a rubber Curate?"

LIFE IS A SEXUALLY TRANSMITTED DISEASE

34

Where does Peter Pan eat?

Wendys!

The young barmaid was ▮▮▮▮▮▮ street
when she ▮▮▮▮▮▮ small boys
▮▮▮▮▮▮ the ▮▮▮▮▮▮
"Whats this ▮▮▮▮▮▮" she asked ▮▮▮▮▮▮
"Its a ▮▮▮▮▮▮" replied the boy.
"Oh, said the barmaid, "▮▮▮▮▮▮?"
"▮▮▮▮▮▮ said the boy, "▮▮▮▮▮▮"

Q. Why do female parachutists always wear tampons?

A. So they don't whistle on the way down!

Overhead at Westminster . . .

. . . when Gerald (Kaufman) becomes *that* pompous and self satisfied I'm very tempted to say:

36

"On the day you were circumcised Gerald, I believe they may have thrown away the wrong end."

Q. What's the difference between Twiggy and a forged dollar?

A. One's a phoney buck, The other's a ...

Definition:

Beer Drinker

A filter between Brewer and Sewer!

37

An Englishman, an Irish... were having dr... into each... rem... ...his— and ...week, he had drunk seventeen

A young couple were soon to be married. But despite repeated attempts on her part the husband to be would not introduce her to his parents.

"My parents are both deaf and mute," he said.

But she still insisted that they must meet.

38

Finally he gave in and they drove over.

"You go straight in," he said, "the door's always open."

"I'll get out the luggage and lock up."

She pushed open the door and froze.

Mother was sitting, stark naked legs wide apart, with a beer bottle up her fanny!

Dad, too, was exposed. Shaking his testicles in cupped hand he was poking a matchstick into his eye!

Naturally our fiancee fled back to the car and in her husband's arms, demanded an answer.

"Oh, they're having a row," he said.

39

"She's saying — get the beers in you cunt.

"He's saying — Bollocks, I'm watching the match."

Michael Davidson — West Ham.

Three Hell's Angels were sitting at a table in a transport cafe.

A nun came in and took the spare seat and began to eat.

Astonished, one of them said, "I went to my parent's wedding last week and we all got rat-arsed."

Catching on the second one said, "My dad says that he will marry my mum next year."

Despite all of this the nun stayed right where she was.

In desperation the third tough said, "My old man says he's never gonna marry mum."

They all looked at the nun who said:

"Would one of you bastards pass the salt please?"

Definition:

Indefinitely

When your balls are slapping against her bum, it's in definitely!

Q.

Whaddya call a black hitchhiker?

41

A.

Stranded!

Bill:
Flobalob, flobalob, flobalob

Ben:
You're supposed to swallow it you prat!

This stuck up woman said to me,

"I don't go to bed with a guy unless he's got a twelve inch cock!"

Quick as a flash I said, "I don't cut off two inches for anybody!"

Q.

What's the difference between a pregnant girl and a light bulb?

A.

You can unscrew a light bulb!

Q.

How does a Jewish hooker get her fur?

A.

Hole Sale!

Q. What goes into thirteen twice?

A. Roman Polanski!

Q. What's the definition of eternity?

A. It's the time between the moment you come and she goes!

43

Bless this food, Oh Lord Divine,
Who changes water into wine.
And also Lord, those worthy men,
Who now will change it back again.

Pamela Todd — London

44

Q.

What's the ideal date?

A.

A blonde nymphomaniac
who turns into a pizza
and a six-pack
at midnight!

Definition:

Foreign Aid

The poor people in rich countries giving money to the rich people in poor countries.

45

A white man stood in a gents toilet ~~glanced~~ and glance down at the ~~co~~ who was standing ~~~~.

"M~~~~ he exclaimed in admiration. "How do you blokes manage to get such ~~big ones~~?"

"~~~~" s~~ai~~d ~~the black man~~. When w~~e~~ a~~re~~ ~~~~ our m~~oth~~ers t~~ie a piece of~~ strin~~g to~~ our tool, the~~y then att~~ch a ~~heavy~~ stone to the string. Eventually that stretches our cocks."

"~~Do y~~ou ~~kn~~ow, I think I'll try that!" announced the white ma~~n~~.

A couple of month~~~~ ~~~~ ag~~~~ the same toilet.

Q.

What part of Popeye never gets rusty?

A.

The part he keeps in Olive Oil!

46

Definition:

Fuck off:

The tiebreaker in an Italian beauty contest!

AT LAST SOME SENSE IS BREAKING THROUGH

Q. What's a lesbian?

A. Just another woman trying to do a man's job!

47

Definition:

Australia

The biggest working men's club in the world.

At the end of a holiday cruise, Mum and her youngest boy leave the docks in a taxi.

His face is pressed to the side window — curious about the women in the doorways.

"What are those women doing Mum — in all the doorways?"

"They're waiting for their husbands to come home — they're probably sailors wives" said Mum.

48

Turning round, the Taxi Driver chipped in; "Be honest with him lady — those ain't wives, they're whores son."

There was a moment's silence and then the boy said: "Do whores have children too Mummy?"

"I suppose they must dear — Taxi Drivers must come from somewhere!"

Peter Barker — Bury St. Edmunds.

"Have you ever found the serial number on a condom?"

"I guess you've never rolled it back that far!

Then there was this chap standing at the bar. Next to him, was a beautifully groomed Old English sheepdog.

A girl in the pub remarked on how lovely the dog was.

"He's a big boy" said the man, "but he's really just a puppy. I still have to teach him everything."

50

"What kind of things?" she asked.

"Well, tricks mostly. At the moment he is learning to fuck women."

Startled and blushing she said: "I don't believe you."

"Meet me in the car park and I'll show you," said the dog's owner.

Minutes later there they were in the car park.

"You take your panties off, spread your legs, bend over my car bonnet and lift your skirt."

This she did
(as she only would in a story!)

And our dog trainer went to work.

"Go on Rover — get in there!"

The dog just looked at him.

"Go on Rover — get in there!"

Still the dog just looked at him.

And the girl was doing her best to be inviting.

"OK Rover," he said, unzipping his flies, "but this is the last time I'm going to show you!"

51

Q.

Did you hear about the
Irish lesbian?

A.

She's into guys!

Q. How do you recognise
an Irish rape suspect?

A. He steps out of the
police line-up and
says:

"That's the girl!"

Q. Did you hear about the Irishman who went to Vegas?

A. He lost all his money in the parking meters!

Q.

What did Donald Duck say to the hooker?

A.

"Put it on my bill!"

53

Q. What's the difference between looking for a lost golf ball and Lady Godiva?

54 ▶

A. One is a hunt on a course . . .

Q. What's strong, white and totally useless on a woman?

A. An Irishman!

Q. What's twelve inches long and white?

A. Nothing!

55

Standing side by side in the lavatory,

The white guy just couldn't help noticing the black tool next to him.

Two feet long and four inches thick, with a string of pearls around the middle!

56

"My God, I've never seen anything in my life that looks like that" said the white guy.

The negro smiled appreciatively and said "Yeah well, there's really nothing else you can wear with black."

Definition:

Jewish dilemma:

A half-priced offer on the bacon!

Q.

Whaddya get when you cross LSD with a birth control pill?

57

A.

A trip without the kids!

JOKES YOU WOULDN'T . . .

Disgusting

58

Q. Whaddya call a Nigerian
with no arms and legs?

A. Trustworthy!

Q. What do gays use
condoms for?

A. To pack their lunch!

Rastus and Lulabelle had just been married and arrived at their new home.

"Lulabelle," said Rastus, "Ah's worried ah might hurt you with my big black dick."

"Rastus you won't hurt me, ah can take anything. Now don't be so silly," said Lulabelle as she undressed and got into bed.

Rastus was still worried, so he took out his dick and poked six inches around the bedroom door. "Is you sure it won't hurt you?"

59

"Sure ah's sure, ah can take anything."

Rastus poked another six inches around the door, "Is you sure Lulabelle?"

"Sure ah's sure, ah can take anything."

"OK Lulabelle, ah's coming up those stairs!"

Q. How does Snow White get seven inches?

A. An inch at a time!

Q.

How do you sink an Italian submarine?

A.

Put it in the water!

60

Q. What's red and has seven dents?

A. Snow White's cherry!

WHADDYA CALL:

A gay guy from Tokyo?

A Japansie!

Definition:

JEWISH foreplay:

Two hours of begging and pleading.

This one is just too tasteless.

Ed.

Q. Why is Jewish divorce
so expensive?

A. Because it's worth it!

Q.

Why do Jewish men
die before their wives?

62

A.

Because they want to!

Q. Why did God give
Negroes rhythm?

A. 'Cause he fucked up
their hair!

Col. Blimp: "I say — did you hear about Carruthers?"

Alestaire: "Joined the Gurkhas didn't he?"

Col. Blimp: "O Lord No! The East African Rifles."

Alestaire: "I thought they were all black?"

Col. Blimp: "No dear boy — only the privates."

Alestaire: "Oh God — how exotic!"

63

A white man, stood in a gents toilet ... ated to glance down at the cock of the black guy ... was standing next to him.

"M... he ex... said ... do... you bl... ... to ... ...

"Y... said ne ... ... When ... are young ou... ... a piece of ... to our tool, and the... ey attach ... stone to the string. Eventua... ... stretches our cocks."

64 ▶

If she married a Pole, what would she get that's long and hard on her wedding night?

A NEW LAST NAME!

A 90-year-old man goes to a hooker.
When he gets undressed,
she looks at his flaccid penis and says,
"Mister, you've had it!"
"Thank you very much" he says.
"How much do I owe you?"

Why are men smarter than women?

65

Because they have two heads!

On their 25th wedding anniversary Solly and his wife had a romantic dinner together.

"You've been such a good wife to me Ruth, is there anything you would *really* like from me?"

"Solly, when we married you insisted that we each had a locked drawer. As a special treat will you let me see what you keep in yours?"

True to his word, Solly opened his private drawer. Inside Ruth found four golf balls and £800 in fivers.

"But what does this mean, Solly? I don't understand."

"Well dearest, I'm afraid that whenever I was unfaithful I put a golf ball in my drawer!"

"Well, I suppose after 25 years, just four isn't too bad. But what about the £800?"

"Well, every time I got up to a dozen I sold them for a fiver!"

A lady tells her doctor:

"Every time I sneeze, I have an orgasm."

"What are you taking for it?" he says.

"Pepper!"

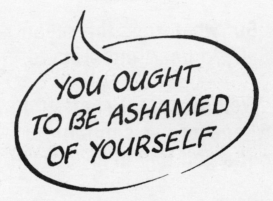

YOU OUGHT
TO BE ASHAMED
OF YOURSELF

68

The young barmaid was ▓▓▓▓▓▓▓▓▓▓ street
when she ▓▓▓▓▓▓▓▓▓▓▓▓▓ small boys
▓▓▓▓▓▓▓▓▓ the ▓▓▓▓▓▓▓
"what's this ▓▓▓▓▓▓?" she asked ▓▓▓▓▓
▓▓▓▓▓
"It's a ▓▓▓▓▓▓" replied the boy.
"Oh, said the barmaid, ▓▓▓▓▓▓▓▓?"
"▓▓▓▓▓▓▓ said the boy, ▓▓▓▓▓▓▓"

**Why did God give
women a vagina?**

So men would talk to them!

69

Definition:

IRISH foreplay

"Brace yourself Maggie!"

Definition:

BLACK foreplay

"Scream and I'll kill you!"

**A guy
walked into the doctor's office,
stuck out his nine inch tongue,
and the nurse said: "Aaaahhhh!"**

70

A white man stood in a gents toilet, ~~happened~~ to glance down at the ~~cock of a black guy~~ who was standing ~~next to him.~~

"M~~y word!~~" he exclaimed in admiration. "How do you blokes manage to get such big ones?"

"~~Well,~~" said the black man. "When we are young our mothers tie a piece of string to our tool, and the ~~other end they attach~~ a heavy stone to the string. Eventually that stretches our cocks."

"~~Do you know,~~ I think I'll try that!" announced the white man.

A couple of months ~~later they met~~ ag~~ain in the same~~ toilet.

Two South Africans were drinking in a bar when a large black man walked in and ordered a drink.

"I'll never get used to that" said one of them.

"That," said the other "is Marvin Hagler, the boxer."

"I bet you fifty bucks it isn't!" said his pal.

"You're on!" said the other, "I'll prove it, I'll ask him who he is and if it's Hagler, I'll get his autograph. Then you can pay up!"

He walked across the bar and had a brief conversation with the black man who suddenly stood up and hit him so hard that he flew across the room and landed in front of his mate.

71

"There you are!", he muttered through broken teeth, "I told you it was Hagler."

"What the hell did you say to him?"

"I just asked him who he was and he said 'I'm Marvellous Marvin Hagler, I'm the Champion of the World, I've got fifty million Dollars and I fuck white women!'"

"So why did he hit you?"

"Dunno. All I said was: 'If I had fifty million Dollars I wouldn't fuck bloody Kaffirs either!'"

What's the difference
between worry and panic?

Worry is the 1st time
you can't do it a 2nd time!

Panic is the 2nd time
you can't do it a 1st time!

Maggie put 'Rest in Peac̶e̶ ....sbands tombstone.
Bꞵut when sꞏ........... boasting about
he had .... went down.
producin............. can see that
clotohin............. greeted by
he had le............. Please stop
told the st............ .....rds that
'Till I com............ .....ained nothing
much use

*This one is
just too
tasteless.
Ed.*

73

WHADDYA CALL

A black necktie salesman?

A tie-coon!

Q. What is the penalty for
   bigamy?

A. Two mothers-in-law.

SEXIST

74

AT LAST SOME
SENSE IS
BREAKING THROUGH

Q. Why does an elephant
have four feet?

A. Six inches wouldn't work!

Yet another woman told me, "I want you to give me nine inches and make it hurt!"

So I stuffed her three times and punched her in the mouth!

76

A motorist was pulled over by a police car in the middle of the night. "I stopped you sir," said the copper, "because one of your rear lights seem to be defective." "Oh, I'm sorry about that," said the motorist, "It's just a bad earth connection." He kicked the tail-lamp which lit up immediately. "Very impressive sir," said the copper, "And I suppose if I were to thump your windscreen, a valid tax-disc would pop up!"

America's richest man was found shot dead today.

His wife described his condition as satisfactory.

Q.

77

What do you call two Irish gays?

A.

Patrick Fitzgerald
and
Gerald Fitzpatrick

Man:
"Doctor! For the last six months my wife's been saying she's a hen."

Doctor:
"Well be firm with her and tell her to pull herself together."

Man:
"But Doctor, we need the eggs."

Priest:
"Tell me Rabbi, when are you going to weaken and eat a nice slice of ham?"

Rabbi:
"At your wedding Father."

*Then there was the
Irish Kamikaze pilot*

*Got a medal for
five successful missions!*

79

Patient: "Doctor I am worried that my
husband may be becoming impotent."

Doctor: "How old is your husband?"

Patient: "Eighty one."

Doctor: "When did you first notice that he
may be losing his potency?

Patient: "Well I first noticed it last night but
what really worries me is that I noticed it
again this morning."

Three prostitutes were off duty, drinking together in a bar.

First Prostitute — with some pride:
"My cunt is now so big I can get a fist in it!"

Second Prostitute — with a superior air:
"You've got a way to go girl, I can now get two fists up!"

Third Prostitute — confidently and rather smugly:
"If you're going to brag dearie, then make sure you've got something to brag about"

Whereupon she spread her legs and slid 12 inches down the bar stool!

80

AND THIS SHOULD HAVE BEEN CENSORED TOO!

81

Definition:
Death

Nature's way of telling you to slow down!

Q. How do you put a Jewish girl off having sex?

82

A. Marry her.

The young barmaid was ~~━━━━━━~~ street
when she ~~━━━━━━~~ small boys
~~━━━━━━~~ the ~~━━━~~
"Whats this ~~━━━~~ ?" she asked ~~━~~
~~━~~
"It's a ~~━━━~~" replied the boy.
"Oh, said the barmaid, ~~━━━━━~~"
"~~━━━━~~ 'said the boy, ~~━━━━~~"

A quiet little guy walked into a brothel and asked to see the madame.

"I am not sure you will be able to help me," he said.

"I want it a special way."

"You go with Lulu and tell her how you want it. She will certainly accommodate you."

Two minutes later he was back.

"Lulu wouldn't do it," he said.

"Go with Fifi then she will do it any way you want it," said madame.

Two minutes later he was back again.

"Fifi wouldn't hear of it," he said.

"I thought I had heard them all," said the madame.

"I had better see to you myself.

Now tell me how you want it

and I promise you that you will get it."

"I want it on credit."

Abie: "Sara, I have tried to be a good husband but I have to tell you that unless I can find five thousand pounds by tomorrow, I will go bankrupt."

Sara: "Abie, in the drawer beside the bed you will find six thousand pounds. I have saved this by putting ten pounds in there every time you made love to me."

84

Abie: "Sara, if only you had told me this before, I would have given you all of my business."

A white man, stood in a gents toilet, chanced to glance down at the cock of the black guy who was standing next to him.

"M_ _ _ he ex_ _ _ _ _ _ _ _ _ _ _ _ _ d_ _ _ u bl_ _ _ _ _ _ _ _ _ _ _ _ _ _ cs'

"Y_ _, said _ _ _ _ _ _ _ _ _. When _ _ are young ou_ _ _ _ _ _ _ _ piece of _ _ _ ng to our tool, and the_ _ _ y attach _ _ _ avy stone to the string. Eve_ _ _ _ _ _ al stretches our cocks."

Somebody once challenged Dorothy Parker to use the word *horticulture* in a sentence.

Quick as a wink she replied:

85

"You can lead a horticulture, but you can't make her think."

Three quiz contestants await the next question. An Englishman, a German and a Frenchman.

"To produce arousal, there are three places to kiss a woman," said the quiz master.

"Which would you kiss first?"

"On the lips," cried the Englishman.

"Correct," said the quizmaster.

86

"Where then the second kiss?" he asked.

"On the neck!" exclaimed the German.

"And where the third then?" he asked.

There was a rather long pause.

Finally the Frenchman spoke up:

"Don't look at me — I've been wrong twice already!"

Q.
What's the difference between a virgin and a light bulb?

A.
You can unscrew a light bulb.

Definition:
hors de combat
Camp followers.

Father O'Malley was just relaxing for the evening when one of his parishioners came knocking at his door. He had with him a parrot in a cage.

"Father, I need your help," he said. "I have to go away for a few days and I need someone to look after my bird Fifi. I know you have parrots of your own, so you're the only person I could think of."

"Michael, I've heard about that bird of yours, it uses some pretty filthy language, My two on the other hand are good devout Catholic parrots that do nothing but pray all day."

"In that case Father, your birds can teach her the error of her ways," said Michael."

"Very well then. Bring her in," said the priest.

Michael carried the bird in and released her into Father O'Malley's aviary where his two birds were perched holding rosaries and muttering 'Hail Mary's'.
Immediately Fifi flew onto a perch and shrieked out, "I wanna fuck! I wanna fuck!"

One of Father O'Malley's parrots immediately dropped his rosary, turned to his companion and squawked, "You can chuck away the beads Charlie. Our prayers have been answered.

Life is like a shit sandwich

The more bread you got, the less shit you eat!

89

I felt about as welcome as:

A pork chop at a jewish barbecue

A turd in the swimming pool

A pork pie in a synagogue

90

Three eminent surgeons in a bar, bragging.

The Australian surgeon boasts of the enormous technical resources and skill in his country. "One day a man was brought to me, crushed so badly that only his arm remained. After weeks of surgery we had rebuilt his body and made it so efficient that it put 50 people out of work."

The American couldn't let that go and he said: "Well let me tell you that we had a guy who'd been caught in a nuclear blast and only his hair was left. We restored the head to it, then the body and he's now put 200 people out of work?"

91

The English surgeon put his glass down: "Well, you both had quite a lot to work with. A couple of years ago, wafting down the corridor, I smelt a fart. I caught it in a jar and took it to surgery. There we wrapped an arsehole round it and then built up a full human body. It was a beautiful job. We called it Norman Lamont and he's put the whole fucking country out of work!"

— R. P. Putney

Definition:
THE GREAT AMERICAN DREAM

All the Blacks swimming back to Africa
With a Puerto Rican under each arm.

92

Q.
What do you call two
Scottish gays?

A.
Ben Dover and
Phil McCrack

The biology master at a girl's school was asking his class questions.

He pointed to the Vicar's daughter .

"Jennifer, tell me which human organ, given the right stimulus, expands to six times its normal size and what stimulus produces this effect?"

"How dare you ask me a question like that?" she said, "I intend to tell my parents.

93

He turned to another girl and said, "You tell me".

"The pupil of the eye in low levels of light," she answered quietly.

Turning back to the Vicar's daughter he said, "I have just two things to say to you: Firstly that you have got a dirty mind, and secondly that one day you are in for a dreadful disappointment."

What are the four most dreaded words in the Yuppie housing estate?

94

Ah's your new neighbour!

Three little boys were sitting on the wall of a big house admiring the cars in the driveway.

The vicar spotted them and said: "If you boys want to own cars like that, you'll have to work hard at school. What do you all want to be when you grow up?"

The first one said: "I wanna be a footballer and have a Ferrari like that one."

The second one said: "I wanna be a Rock Star and have a Rolls like that one."

The third one said: "I wanna be the hairiest man in the world!"

"Whatever for?" said the vicar.

95

"'cos my sister's only got a little bit of hair just between her legs and she said it got her that house and all of those cars!"

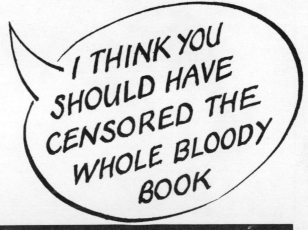

If this book has made you laugh and you want some more, here's another to look for.

JOKES FOR DIRTY, RACIST, SEXIST MEN

It's even funnier — Ed.